■SCHOLASTIC

BEST PRACTICES in Action

Nonfiction
Read & Write Booklets
Animals & Habitats

by Alyse Sweeney

NEW YORK • TORONTO • LONDON • AUCKLAND • SYDNEY
MEXICO CITY • NEW DELHI • HONG KONG • BUENOS AIRES

Teaching Resources

For Mom

Cover design by Brian LaRossa

Cover and interior illustrations by Maxie Chambliss

Interior design by Ellen Matlach for Boultinghouse & Boultinghouse

ISBN-13: 978-0-439-56760-2

ISBN-10: 0-439-56760-2

Copyright © 2007 by Alyse Sweeney

Published by Scholastic Inc.

2 3 4 5 6 7 8 9 10   40   15 14 13 12 11 10 09 08 07

Contents

Nonfiction Read & Write Booklets

Introduction

During the time I was a Scholastic editor, a large part of my job was finding out from primary-grade teachers what materials would be most useful to them in the classroom. Over the years second- and third-grade teachers spoke of the growing need for the following:

- engaging nonfiction texts that tie in to the curriculum

- more opportunities to engage students in meaningful writing

- writing prompts that connect to texts and build higher-order thinking skills

Nonfiction Read & Write Booklets: Animals and Habitats delivers each of these valuable components in an interactive mini-book format. The ten booklets cover key topics about animals and habitats and engage students with lively text, thought-provoking writing prompts, and opportunities to draw. Best of all, when students are finished, they'll have a unique, personalized book to take home and share. The sense of ownership and accomplishment that comes with completing these mini-books is highly motivating.

Each booklet is filled with a variety of nonfiction features and structures to help students learn to navigate informational text. They'll learn key concepts from reading charts, webs, and diagrams. In addition, each mini-book presents students with opportunities to write informational text. After reading a chart, diagram, or short passage, students are asked to infer, evaluate, apply, analyze, compare, explain, or summarize. As a result, children develop critical-thinking skills and gain a deeper understanding of each topic.

Once students have completed their booklets and shared them with classmates, encourage them to share their work with family members. Sending the books home provides families with opportunities to observe and support their children's literacy development as well as discover what topics they are learning about in school.

With these interactive booklets in hand, children reflect upon what they are reading, think critically, develop their own ideas, and express themselves in writing. Nonfiction Read & Write Booklets provide an engaging format for helping students comprehend the features of nonfiction and for satisfying their curiosity about the world around them.

Why Teach Nonfiction?

Research has provided insight into the importance of teaching nonfiction. Here are some key findings:

- Informational text helps students build knowledge of the world around them (e.g., Anderson & Guthrie, 1999; Duke & Kays, 1998, as cited in Duke & Bennett-Armistead, 2003). This can potentially deepen students' comprehension of subsequent texts (e.g., Wilson & Anderson, 1986, as cited in Duke & Bennett-Armistead, 2003).

- Many students struggle with content area reading (Vacca, 2002; Walpole, 1998, as cited in Kristo and Bamford, 2004). Providing students with high-quality nonfiction materials may help better prepare them to meet these challenges.

- Providing students in the lower grades with more exposure to nonfiction may alleviate the decline in achievement often observed in fourth grade (Chall, Jacobs, and Baldwin, 1990; Duke, 2000, as cited in Boynton and Blevins, 2005).

- Exposing students in the early grades to informational texts helps improve their skills as readers and writers of informational text when they are older (Papps, 1991; Sanacore, 1991, as cited in Kristo and Bamford, 2004).

- Studies have shown that some students prefer nonfiction to fiction (Donovan, Smolkin, and Lomax, 2000; Caswell and Duke, 1998, as cited in Boynton and Blevins, 2004). Including more nonfiction materials in your classroom instruction taps into these students' interests and may increase their motivation.

- Teaching students to read nonfiction will give them real-world skills and prepare them for the materials they'll read outside of school. One study found that the text on the World Wide Web is 96 percent expository (Kamil & Lane, 1998, as cited in Duke & Bennett-Armistead, 2003). Students will encounter informational text not only on the Web but also all around them—it's essential that they have the tools to comprehend it.

Connections to the Standards

These books are designed to support you in meeting the following standards outlined by Mid-continent Research for Education and Learning (McREL), an organization that collects and synthesizes national and state standards.

Reading

—Uses the general skills and strategies of the reading process, including:

- Uses meaning clues such as picture captions, title, cover, and headings to aid comprehension.

—Uses reading skills and strategies to understand and interpret a variety of informational texts, including:

- Understands the main idea and supporting details of simple expository information.
- Relates new information to prior knowledge and experience.
- Uses text organizers (e.g., headings, topic and summary sentences, graphic features, typeface) to determine the main ideas and to locate information in a text.
- Understands structural patterns or organization in informational texts (e.g., chronological, logical, or sequential order; compare-and-contrast; cause-and-effect; proposition and support).

Source: *Content Knowledge: A Compendium of Standards and Benchmarks for K–12 Education.* 4th edition. (Mid-continent Research for Education and Learning, 2004)

Writing

—Uses the general skills and strategies of the writing process.

—Uses the stylistic and rhetorical aspects of writing.

—Uses grammatical and mechanical conventions in written compositions.

Geography

—Understands the concept of regions.

- Knows areas that can be classified as regions according to physical criteria and human criteria.

—Understands the characteristics of ecosystems on Earth's surface.

- Knows the components of ecosystems at a variety of scales (e.g., fungi, insects, plants, and animals in a food chain or food web; fish and marine vegetation in coastal zones; grasses, birds, and insects in grassland areas).
- Knows ways in which humans can change ecosystems.
- Knows plants and animals associated with various vegetation and climatic regions on Earth.

How to Use This Book

These booklets can be completed during class or as homework. Before students begin, walk them through each page so that they clearly understand how to respond to the writing prompts and how to read any challenging text features, such as charts or diagrams. If students need additional support, guide them as they work on a section of a booklet. You might have students complete a booklet over the course of several days, working on a few pages at a time.

Activate Prior Knowledge

Introduce each booklet with a discussion that activates students' prior knowledge. Ask students what they know about the topic, what they think they'll learn about the topic from the booklet, and what they would like to learn about the topic.

Walk Through the Booklet

After introducing the booklet and discussing the topic, walk through the pages together to satisfy children's curiosity and clarify the instructions. Point out the writing and drawing prompts and explain to students that although everyone is starting with the same booklet, they will each have a unique book when they are finished.

Read, Write, Draw, and Learn

Read and discuss the text together, pointing out vocabulary words and raising questions. Then move on to the accompanying writing and drawing prompts. Generate possible answers with students. Encourage students to write in complete sentences. Talk about what they learned from a particular section. Were they surprised about something they learned? Do they want to know more about a topic?

Share

At various points in the bookmaking process, have students share their written responses with their classmates. Draw attention to the similarities and differences in their responses. Be sure to send the booklets home for students to share with families. The repeated readings will help children develop fluency.

Extend Learning

On pages 7–8, you'll find two extension activities for each booklet. These will reinforce concepts covered in the books and explore a particular topic in more depth.

How to Assemble the Booklets

It works well to assemble the booklets together as a class.

Directions:

1. Carefully remove the perforated pages from the book.
2. Make double-sided copies of each page on standard 8½- by 11-inch paper.
3. Fold each page in half along the dashed line.
4. Place the pages in numerical order and staple along the spine.

TIP: You may want to have students fill in their books before stapling them. This way the center pages will lie flat while students are writing.

Extension Activities

My Book About Mountain Animals

- On a map, locate the closest mountain range to where you live. Which states are home to this mountain range? Share quick facts about the mountain range, such as its height and climate as well as its animal and plant life. Locate other mountain ranges in the world.

- Pages 3 and 4 of the booklet introduce students to several mountain animals. Lead a discussion about additional mountain animals, such as raccoons, owls, white pelicans, red foxes, elk, deer, mountain sheep, weasels, and marmots. Assign partners to research an animal and share facts with the class.

My Book About Cave Animals

- Discuss the concept web on page 2 and the information about the three zones on pages 3 and 4. Talk about ways to combine the information and show which of the three groups of cave animals live in each of the three cave zones. Encourage students to come up with different charts and graphic organizers to present this information.

- About 100 years ago, a New Mexican cowboy named Jim White saw a huge dark cloud rising up from the ground. He realized that he was looking at hundreds of bats! The next day Jim took a rope and ladder into the hole in the ground where the bats emerged and discovered Carlsbad Caverns. Share this story with your students. Then have them write about what it might be like to discover a cave that is home to thousands of bats.

My Book About Forest Animals

- Use the information on page 6 to create a web showing animals that migrate, hibernate, and stay active in the winter. Label the center of the web "What Forest Animals Do in Winter."

Invite students to do additional research and add to the list of animals in each category. Discuss the fact that information can be presented in different formats. Compare the paragraph format in the booklet with the graphic organizer you created.

- Research and work together to create a chart that describes the job of a forest ranger. (A forest ranger maps forests, records types of plants and wildlife, decides whether trees will be cut down, teaches visitors about forest plants and animals, tests soil and water, and works to keep the soil and water healthy.)

My Book About Desert Animals

- Have students satisfy their curiosity about a chosen desert animal by researching and answering the questions they posed on page 4 of the booklet. Encourage students to share what they learned with classmates.

- On the board, write the names of the deserts in North America. Locate the deserts on a map and pinpoint the states where the deserts are found. Record the information in a graphic organizer or chart.

My Book About Polar Animals

- Discuss the penguin diagram on pages 5 and 6 of the booklet. Then select one or more polar animals that have multiple adaptations for their harsh environment. Draw the animal(s) on chart paper and use call-outs to locate and describe each adaptation. Or you might have students create their own diagrams.

- Read aloud *Do Penguins Get Frostbite? Questions and Answers About Polar Animals,* by Melvin and Gilda Berger (Scholastic, 2001). Which questions are most pressing for students? Have students generate their own questions about polar animals they'd like to research.

My Book About Prairie Animals

- Compare rainfall in different habitats. On chart paper, create a bar graph comparing annual rainfall in four habitats (desert: 10 inches; prairie: 30 inches; rain forest: 90 inches; temperate deciduous forest: 60 inches). Discuss the graph and create math problems, such as "How many more inches of rain fall in the forest than on the prairie each year?"

- Use the information in the chart on page 1 of the booklet to create a three-way Venn diagram. Label the converging center circle "Grass Grows on a Prairie." In each of the three circles, write information describing the three types of prairies.

My Book About Pond Animals

- Create a pond food chain. Have students use their research from page 7 of the booklet to illustrate a simple food chain. The food chain can show the prey and predators of students' chosen pond animal.

- Compare and contrast a pond in the summer and a pond in winter. What happens to the water in both seasons? What happens to the animals? The following books address this topic well: *Pond*, by Gordon Morrison (Houghton Mifflin, 2002), and *Pond Year*, by Kathryn Lasky (Candlewick Press, 1997).

My Book About Rain Forest Animals

- Invite students to illustrate the poem on page 2 of the booklet. How many details from the poem can they include in their drawings?

- Explore picture books that address the tragic situation of today's rain forests and the growing numbers of endangered rain forest animals. Read aloud *The Great Kapok Tree: A Tale of the Amazon Rain Forest*, by Lynne Cherry (Gulliver Green, 1990). Create problem and solution charts with information from this book and other resources.

My Book About Ocean Animals

- Many ocean animals have names that describe how they look. Show pictures of animals such as parrot fish, crown-of-thorns, and rattail fish without telling the names of these creatures. See how close students can come to guessing the animals' names!

- Read aloud *Meet My Grandmother: She's a Deep-Sea Explorer*, by Lisa Tucker McElroy (The Millbrook Press, 2000). Create a graphic organizer that identifies the many aspects of a sea explorer's work, from researching, exploring, and writing about the ocean to talking about the ocean with companies, other scientists, and children in schools across the country.

My Book About Wetland Animals

- Divide the class into groups and have each group make the sounds of a particular frog or toad. For example, a wood frog makes a quacking sound, a woodhouse's toad makes a nasal "baa-baa," a pig frog "oinks," and a bullfrog sounds like it's saying "chug-o-rum" in a deep voice.

- Invite students to use the question they posed about wetland animals on page 2 of the booklet as the focus of their research. Have students share their findings with the class.

Selected References

Boynton, A. & Blevins, W. (2005). *Nonfiction passages with graphic organizers for independent practice: Grades 2–4*. New York: Scholastic.

Boynton, A. & Blevins, W. (2004). *Teaching students to read nonfiction: Grades 2–4*. New York: Scholastic.

Duke, N. K., & Bennett-Armistead, S. V. (2003). *Reading & writing informational text in the primary grades*. New York: Scholastic.

Kristo, J. V., & Bamford, R. A. (2004). *Nonfiction in focus*. New York: Scholastic.

My Book About Mountain Animals

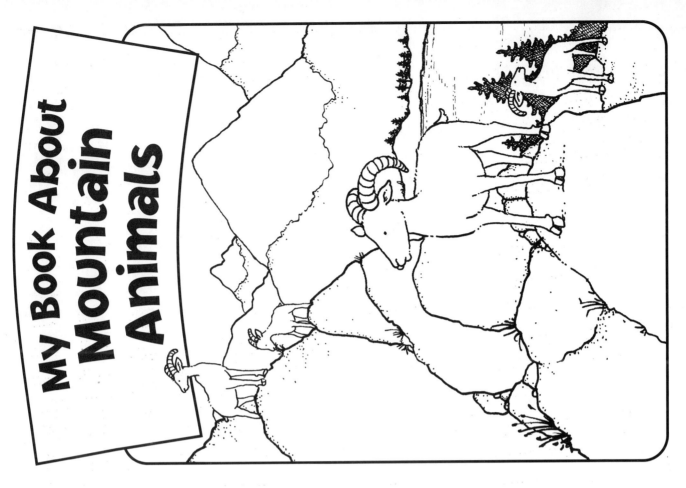

by _____

Animal Spotlight

Which mountain animal would you like to learn more about? Write three questions you have about the animal you chose. Then do research to find the answers to your questions.

Question 1 _____

_____

_____

Answer: _____

_____

Question 2 _____

_____

Answer: _____

_____

Question 3 _____

_____

Answer: _____

7

A Home Reaching Into the Clouds

Have you ever climbed a mountain? If you have, you felt the air become colder the higher you climbed. At a certain height, trees cannot grow because it is too cold, dry, and windy. The highest point where trees can grow is called the **timberline**. Only a few plants can survive above the timberline.

Most animals live on the lower part of a mountain, where there are many trees and plants, as well as water.

Name as many animals as you can that live in the mountains.

1

A mountain goat has **four stomachs** for digesting tough grasses. The stomachs work to get out as many nutrients as possible from each meal.

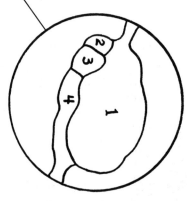

Two layers of hair keep the goat warm when the temperature dips well below zero degrees. The top coat is long and shaggy. The inner coat is short and woolly.

Explain in your own words how these adaptations help the mountain goat survive.

6

timberline

Nonfiction Read & Write Booklets: Animals and Habitats Scholastic Teaching Resources

2

Toughing It Out Above the Timberline

Most animals that live in the high mountains move to lower levels in the winter where it is easier to find food and shelter. Not the mountain goat! How does this amazing animal survive the bitter cold winters?

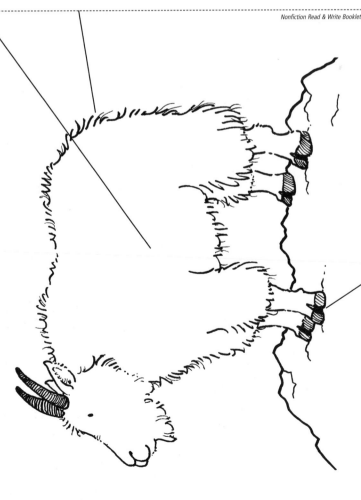

A mountain goat has **split hooves** that spread apart and grip onto rock. The hooves also have soft, rubbery pads that help the goat cling to rock and ice.

5

A Mountain Is Home to . . .

Golden eagles dive from the air, snatching prey such as squirrels and rabbits.

Picas live in groups called colonies.

Grizzly bears sleep during the winter. They live off the fat stored in their bodies.

Quick, strong **wolves** eat moose, elk, deer, small animals, and berries.

Moose have long legs for wading through deep snow.

Snowshoe hares have large back feet with coarse hair on the bottom that keep them from sinking into deep snow.

Describe ways that living on a mountain could be difficult for some animals.

_____

_____

_____

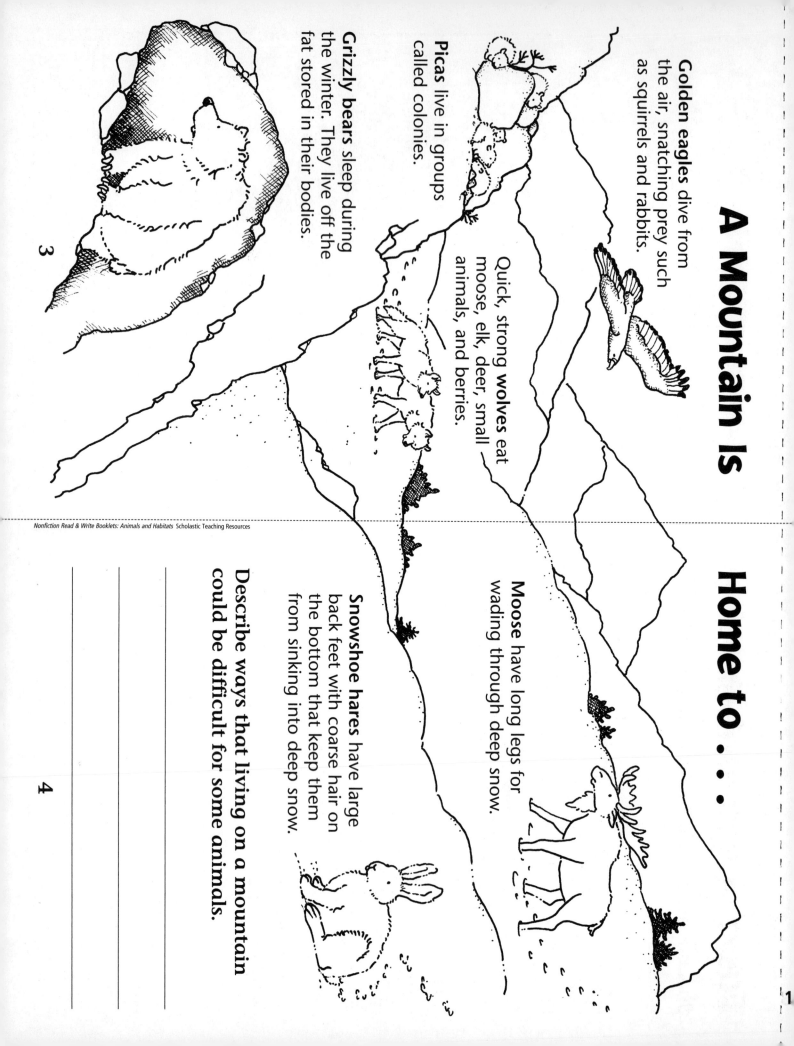

3

4

My Book About Cave Animals

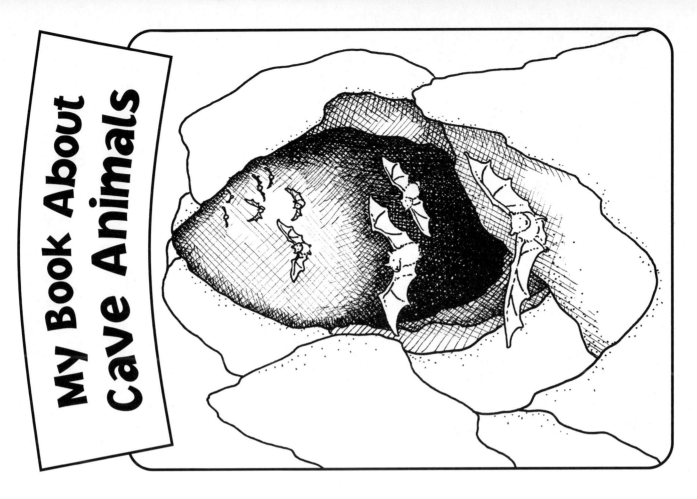

by _____

3

What a Spelunker Sees

Spelunkers are people who explore caves.

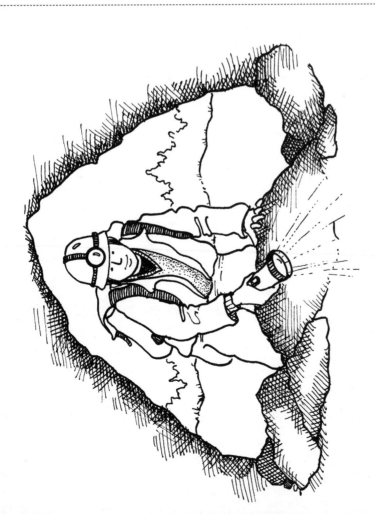

Would you like to be a spelunker?
Why or why not?

_____

_____

_____

7

Incredible Caves

A cave is a dark, hollow space deep in the earth. There are thousands of caves all over the world. Most caves form in a type of rock called **limestone**. Here are other ways caves form:

- in ice
- by waves crashing against a rocky cliff
- by hot running lava

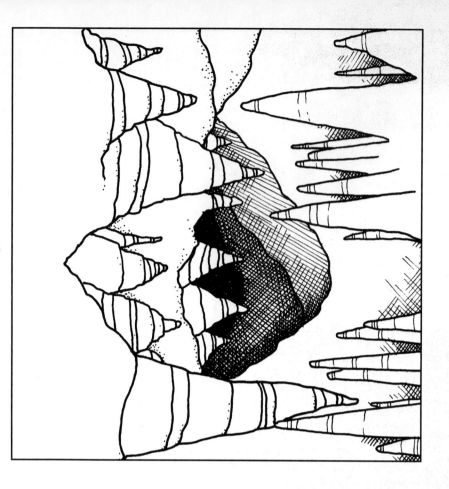

1

Nonfiction Read & Write Booklets: Animals and Habitats Scholastic Teaching Resources

This way of seeing in the dark is called **echolocation**. Echolocation keeps bats from flying into trees, cave walls, and even each other.

People can't hear the clicking noises bats make when they echolocate. But if we could, some would sound as soft as people talking while others would sound as loud as a smoke alarm!

Are you happy that you can't hear bats echolocate, or would you like to hear their loud, quick clicks? Explain your answer.

_____

_____

_____

_____

_____

_____

_____

6

14

Troglophiles
like to live in caves but can make their homes elsewhere.

Examples: spiders, cockroaches, salamanders, cave fish

Trogloxenes
are known as "cave visitors." These animals spend time in caves but cannot survive here year-round.

Examples: bats, skunks, snakes

3 KINDS OF CAVE ANIMALS

Troglobites are the true cave dwellers. They never leave the cave and cannot live anywhere else.

Examples: blind salamanders, blind cave fish, cave crayfish

Each group of animals lives in a different **zone**, or part of the cave. How might the entrance of a cave be different from the middle of a cave?

_____

_____

_____

2

"Click! Click! Got You!"

Bats have a special way of finding insects in the dark.

1. First the bat makes clicking sounds with its mouth or nose.

2. When the sound reaches the insect, an echo bounces back to the bat.

3. The bat can tell where the insect is by the sound of the echo. The bat can even tell the size and shape of the insect by the echo!

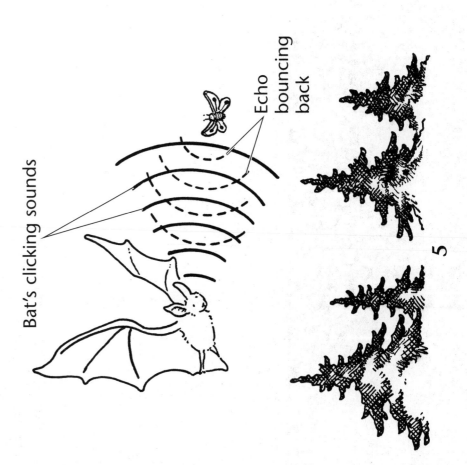

Bat's clicking sounds

Echo bouncing back

5

Inside a Cave

There is a lot of activity in the **entrance zone**. Since there is some sunlight, plants can grow on the cave floor.

In the **twilight zone**, you can still see, but it is darker.

There is no light at all in the **dark zone**. Most animals that live in the dark zone are blind. Some don't even have eyes at all! But their sense of hearing, taste, smell, and touch is quite strong.

Bears sleep in caves in the winter months.

Cave swallows build nests in the warm cave rocks.

During the day, **bats** hang upside down and sleep. At night, they leave the cave to eat insects.

Owls also leave the cave to hunt at night.

Salamanders dart around the rocks of the cave's entrance.

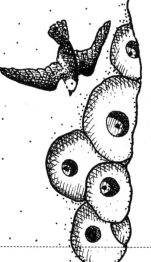

During the day, pack **rats** live in the cave. At night, they leave the cave to look for food.

Cave spiders eat guano—the solid waste of bats.

How have animals living in the dark zone adapted to their environment?

cave crayfish

blind salamander

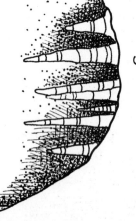

blind cave fish

My Book About Forest Animals

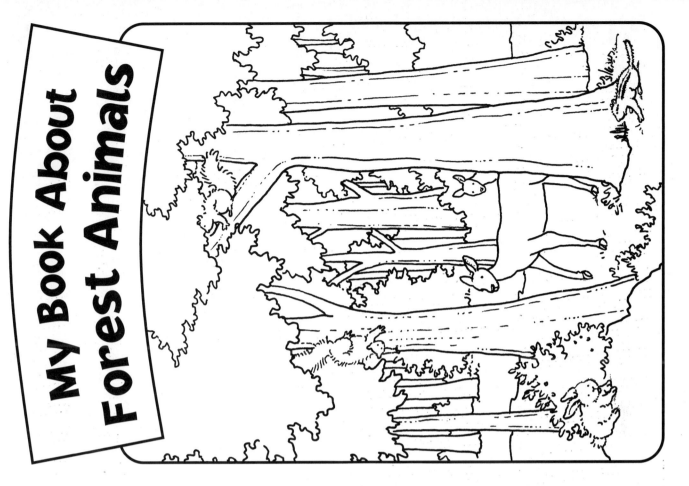

by _____

Save a Tree!

Did you know that every time you use both sides of a piece of paper you help save a tree? That's because trees are cut down to make paper. Remember that animals make their homes in trees.

In the tree, draw three forest animals that are eating, sleeping, hunting, or hiding.

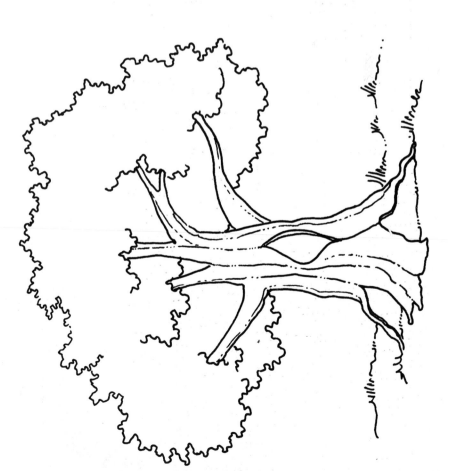

7

Welcome to the Forest!

When you think of a forest, do you picture this kind of forest? ......→

Or this kind of forest? ......→

Or maybe you picture a forest that looks like this? ......→

Or this? ......→

There are different kinds of forests, and each is home to many kinds of animals.

Think about what you already know about forests. What might you see, smell, and hear as you walk through a deep, dark forest?

_____

_____

_____

_____

1

In the winter, most birds and some butterflies **migrate**, or move, to warmer climates. Other forest animals **hibernate**, or go into a deep sleep. Woodchucks, snakes, and ladybugs hibernate. Bears, raccoons, and chipmunks spend a lot of time sleeping, but they wake from time to time to eat.

Other animals stay active and deal with the cold the best they can. Deer, foxes, bobcats, weasels, rabbits, and some birds can all be seen out and about in winter.

Would you want to be a forest animal that migrates, hibernates, or stays active? Why?

_____

_____

_____

_____

6

Types of Forests

		Description
Temperate Deciduous Forest	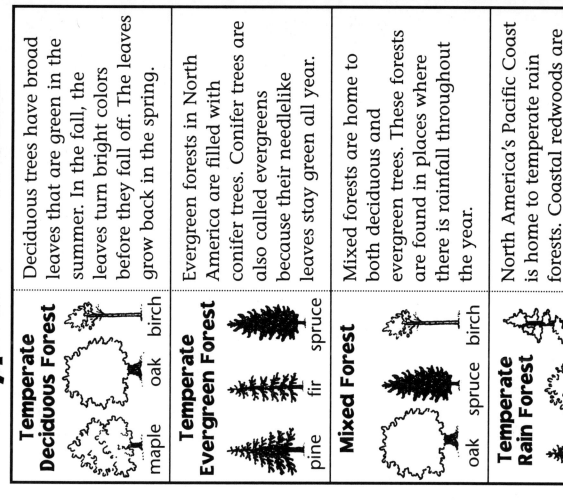 maple oak birch	Deciduous trees have broad leaves that are green in the summer. In the fall, the leaves turn bright colors before they fall off. The leaves grow back in the spring.
Temperate Evergreen Forest	pine fir spruce	Evergreen forests in North America are filled with conifer trees. Conifer trees are also called evergreens because their needlelike leaves stay green all year.
Mixed Forest	oak spruce birch	Mixed forests are home to both deciduous and evergreen trees. These forests are found in places where there is rainfall throughout the year.
Temperate Rain Forest	fir cottonwood redwood	North America's Pacific Coast is home to temperate rain forests. Coastal redwoods are the world's tallest trees. Giant sequoias are not as tall, but they are wider.

2

Nonfiction Read & Write Booklets: Animals and Habitats Scholastic Teaching Resources

Winter in the Forest

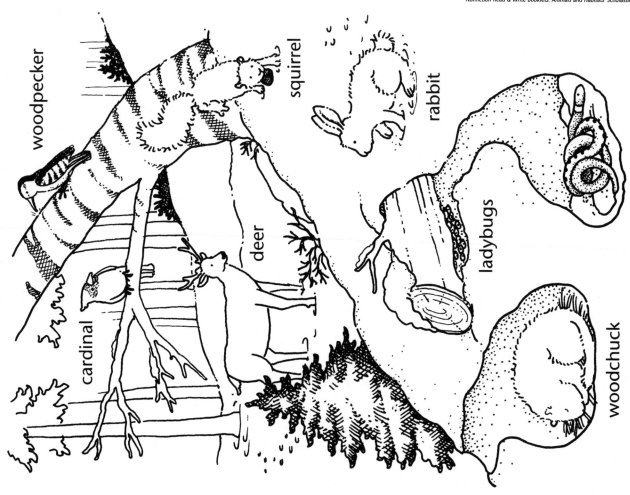

woodpecker

squirrel

rabbit

cardinal

deer

ladybugs

ring-necked snake

woodchuck

5

A Woodland Forest Is

Woodpeckers drill holes in trees, searching for beetles and other insects to eat.

Raccoons hunt at night. They rest in tree holes during the day.

Spotted fawns are hard to see in the sun-speckled forest.

Young **foxes** spend their first three months in a den, such as a hollow log.

3

Home to . . .

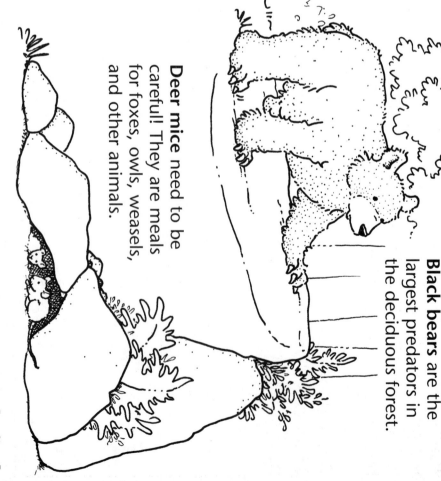

Black bears are the largest predators in the deciduous forest.

Deer mice need to be careful! They are meals for foxes, owls, weasels, and other animals.

Describe two examples of how animals find protection in their forest home.

_____

_____

_____

4

My Book About Desert Animals

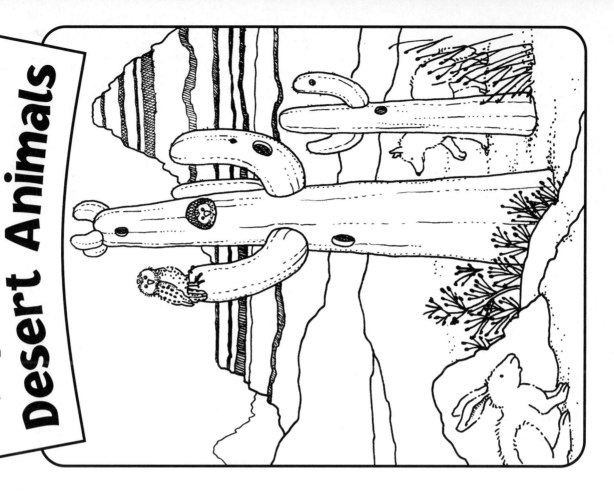

by _____

1

A Day in the Desert

You're off to explore the desert today! The temperature is 110 degrees Fahrenheit. What will you pack? Will you bring a camera or binoculars? A pencil and notebook?

Draw the items you will take with you. Then describe how you'll spend your day in the desert.

7

What Is a Desert?

Which statement is true?
a. All deserts are hot.
b. All deserts are dry.
c. All deserts are sandy.

The answer:
b. All deserts are dry.

Some deserts are hot and some deserts are sandy. Yet many are not. All deserts are dry. They get very little rain.

1

Think about what you learned in this diagram. Explain what the word *adaptation* means.

_____

_____

How has the camel adapted to living in the desert?

A camel can close its nostrils to keep out sand.

With tough skin on its lips and strong teeth, a camel can eat sharp, pointy desert plants without a problem.

_____

_____

_____

_____

_____

_____

_____

6

22

Comparing Deserts

The Sonoran Desert (southwestern United States)

Huge saguaro cacti live here.

The Sahara (North Africa)

Tall sand dunes stretch for miles.

All of these deserts are dry.

The Desert of the Colorado Plateau (southwestern United States)

Long ago, water shaped the colorful rock into interesting shapes.

Different animals live in different deserts. Why do you think this is so?

_____

_____

_____

2

Nonfiction Read & Write Booklets: Animals and Habitats Scholastic Teaching Resources

A Sahara Superstar

How does the camel get by in the hot, sandy Sahara? Read the diagram to learn about the camel's amazing adaptations.

A camel lives on fat stored in its hump when there is no other food to eat.

Thick hair on its head, neck, throat, and hump protect the camel from sunburn.

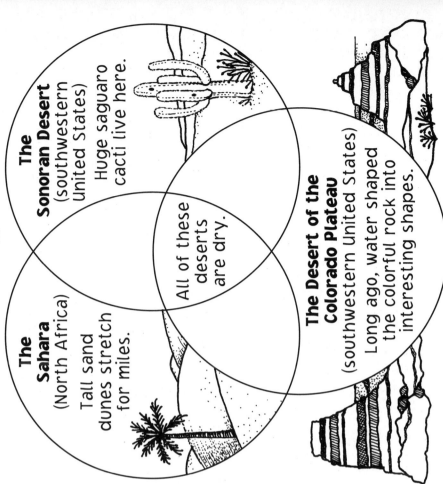

Hair inside its ears and long eyelashes keep out blowing sand.

Thick pads on its feet spread out and keep the camel from sinking in the sand.

5

The Sonoran Desert

Coyotes are omnivores, which means they eat almost anything.

Jackrabbits stay cool as heat from their bodies escapes through their large ears.

Gila monsters are poisonous lizards that spend hot days underground.

Kangaroo rats get all the water they need from seeds and other food.

3

Nonfiction Read & Write Booklets: Animals and Habitats Scholastic Teaching Resources

Is Home to . . . .

Wild pigs, called javelinas, travel in groups. They eat cacti and plant roots.

The poisonous **scorpion** stays cool under rocks during the day and hunts at night.

Which one of these desert animals would you like to learn more about?

Write three questions you have about this animal.

1. _____

2. _____

3. _____

4

My Book About Polar Animals

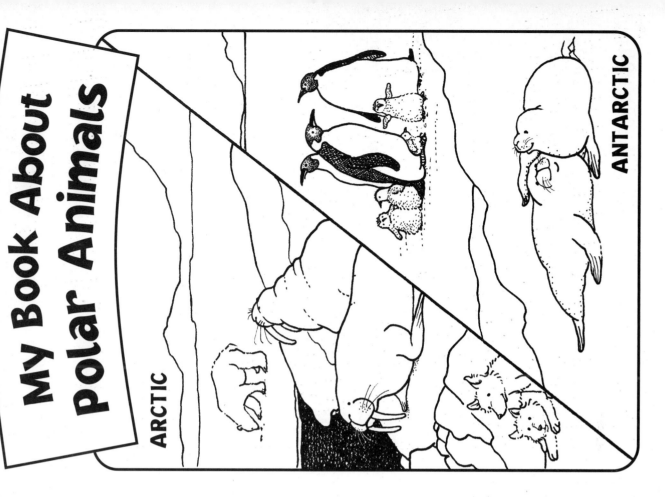

ARCTIC

ANTARCTIC

by _____

5

Protect Polar Animals!

Polar bears, walruses, whales, and other polar animals have been overhunted. Today, there are laws to protect these creatures.

Draw a picture of an overhunted polar animal (from the list above or from your research). Then explain why it's important to protect this animal.

7

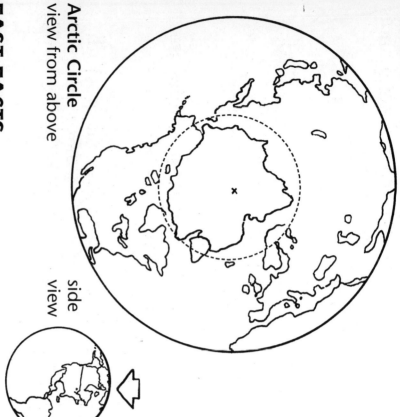

Arctic Circle
view from above

side
view

FAST FACTS

- The Arctic region is made up of:
  ✓ an ice-covered ocean called the Arctic Ocean
  ✓ treeless land called **tundra** on the north edges of North America, Asia, and Europe
- If you swam in Arctic water, you would freeze in two minutes.
- In the Arctic region, the sun shines only from March to September.

1

Nonfiction Read & Write Booklets: Animals and Habitats Scholastic Teaching Resources

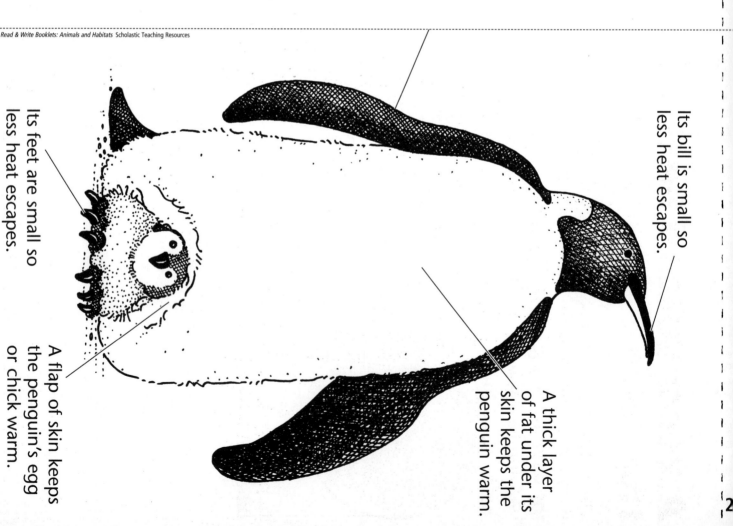

Its bill is small so less heat escapes.

A thick layer of fat under its skin keeps the penguin warm.

Its feet are small so less heat escapes.

A flap of skin keeps the penguin's egg or chick warm.

6

2

Polar bears are the largest and strongest land animals in the Arctic.

Walruses use their tusks to dig up shellfish.

Baby **beluga whales** are called calves.

Arctic foxes have air in their hair. The air keeps the heat close to the fox's body.

Write a fun fact about another Arctic animal. Draw a picture of the animal in the box.

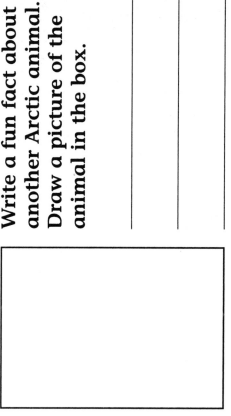

2

Nonfiction Read & Write Booklets: Animals and Habitats Scholastic Teaching Resources

A Body Built to Beat the Cold

The emperor penguin is well adapted to living year-round in the bitter cold. Read the diagram to see how this amazing animal does it.

Oily feathers keep water away from the penguin's skin. The feathers overlap like roof shingles to keep out cold air. As many as 70 feathers would fit on a postage stamp!

Explain in your own words what this diagram tells us about penguins.

5

7

The Antarctic

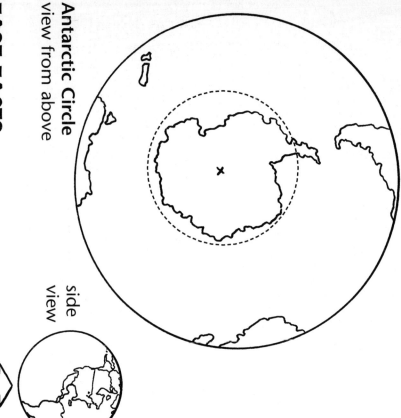

Antarctic Circle
view from above

side
view

FAST FACTS

- The Antarctic is a frozen continent.
- The Antarctic is the coldest place on Earth. The average winter temperature there is 76 degrees Fahrenheit below zero.
- Some parts of the Antarctic are buried in ice that is about three miles thick!
- Few animals live here in the winter. Many come in the summer when there is lots of food and it's safe to nest and raise young.

3

The blue whale is the largest animal that has ever lived. It weighs more than 25 elephants.

Emperor penguins are the largest of 17 kinds of penguins. They live in large groups called colonies.

The **Weddell seal** spends much of the winter in water under the Antarctic ice. When it needs to breathe, it sticks its nose through a crack in the ice.

Antarctic ice fish have special blood that doesn't freeze in ice-cold water.

Write a fun fact about another Antarctic animal. **Draw a picture of the animal in the box.**

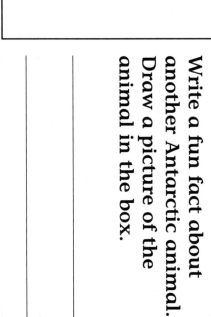

4

2

My Book About Prairie Animals

by _____

Protect the Prairies!

Today only small areas of prairie are left. Conservation groups buy prairie land to prevent towns or farms from being built there.

Explain why these groups might think it's important to protect the prairies. Draw a picture to illustrate your writing.

7

A Sea of Grass

On a prairie, you can see grass for miles and miles. That's why prairies are also called grasslands. Many animals live among the grass and wildflowers.

Three Types of North American Prairie

Short-Grass Prairie	Mixed-Grass Prairie	Tall-Grass Prairie
• located in the western part of the Midwest, where there is little rain	• located in the middle part of the Midwest	• located in the eastern part of the Midwest, where there is lots of rain
• the grass is short and doesn't grow taller than knee-high	• both tall and short grasses grow here	• grass can grow taller than an adult

---

Nonfiction Read & Write Booklets: Animals and Habitats Scholastic Teaching Resources

Describe how a burrow is similar to a person's home.

_____

_____

_____

Describe how a burrow differs from a person's home.

_____

_____

_____

_____

_____

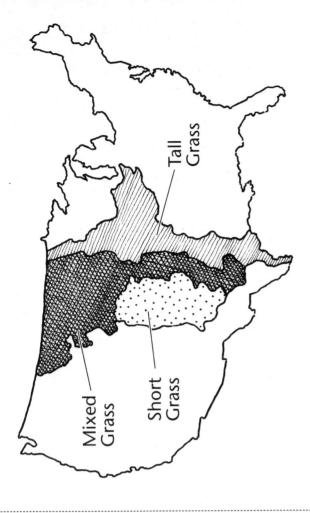

Tall Grass

Mixed Grass

Short Grass

Read the chart on page 1 carefully. Why do you think tall grass grows in the eastern part of the Midwest while short grass grows in the western part?

_____

_____

_____

_____

List as many prairie animals as you can.

_____

2

Why burrow?

A burrow keeps animals warm in the cold winter.

A burrow protects animals from predators.

A burrow keeps animals cool in the hot summer.

A burrow protects animals from strong winds.

5

1

A Prairie Is Home to . . . .

Pronghorn antelopes are the fastest animals on the prairie—and in North America!

Coyotes are the largest predators on the prairie. They eat rabbits, goats, and sheep.

Prairie dogs live in large colonies called towns.

What else do you know about these or other prairie animals?

_____

_____

_____

Nonfiction Read & Write Booklets: Animals and Habitats Scholastic Teaching Resources

Turkey vultures are scavengers, or animals that feed on dead animals.

American bison used to roam in huge herds before settlers arrived. They are also called buffalo.

Burrowing owls make their home in empty prairie dog burrows.

Which animal would you like to learn more about? Why?

_____

_____

My Book About Pond Animals

by _____

Animal Spotlight

Choose a pond animal you'd like to learn more about. Draw a picture of the animal. Then write about it below.

_____ eats _____.
(pond animal)

Something interesting I learned about this creature is:

_____

_____

_____

7

Life in a Pond

A pond is a small area of shallow, still water. Sometimes pond water looks green. That's because large amounts of tiny plants called **green algae** grow easily in pond water. Algae and other plants are the only pond life that makes food directly from sunlight.

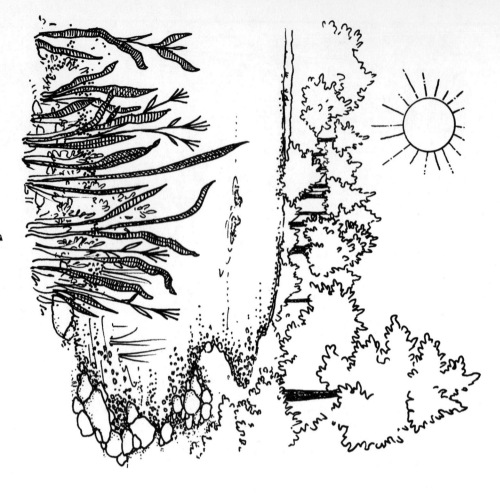

Each of the four strong **wings** can move by themselves. This allows the dragonfly to hover in the air, turn quickly, and fly backward.

The **thorax** is the large body part that contains the main organs.

Each huge **eye** has about 30,000 lenses, allowing the dragonfly to see very well.

Claws at the ends of the **feet** help the dragonfly grip wet and slippery surfaces.

Small, spiky **hairs** on the legs help the dragonfly hold on to its food.

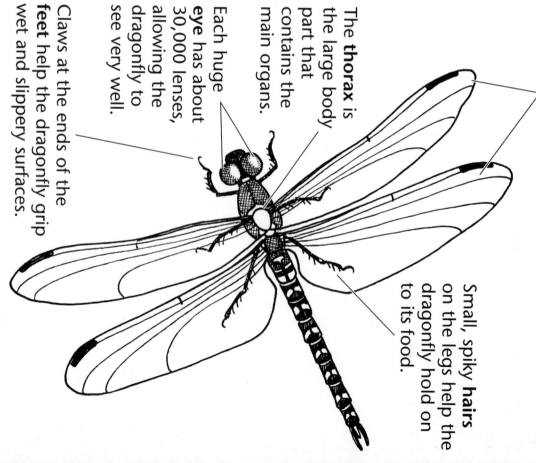

Green algae and other plants are the beginning of a pond food chain.

Tadpoles eat algae.

Green algae

Fish eat tadpoles.

Belted kingfishers eat fish.

Explain how pond animals are all connected to one another in the food chain.

2

Nonfiction Read & Write Booklets: Animals and Habitats Scholastic Teaching Resources

It's a Dragonfly!

Dragonflies have been around for millions of years. This beautiful insect, which once flew alongside dinosaurs, can be seen today flying around ponds and hunting other insects.

After reading the diagram, explain what makes the dragonfly such a good hunter.

5

A Pond Is Home to . . .

When young **wood ducklings** are ready to leave their nest in a tree, they jump right into the pond!

Pumpkinseed fish protect their offspring until they can take care of themselves.

Female **bullfrogs** lay thousands of eggs at a time.

Beavers build lodges that have one or more underwater openings.

Painted box turtles eat plants as well as fish, snails, and insects.

A **water boatman** has back legs that look like oars.

Sadly, many ponds today are littered with trash. How might trash affect the animals living there?

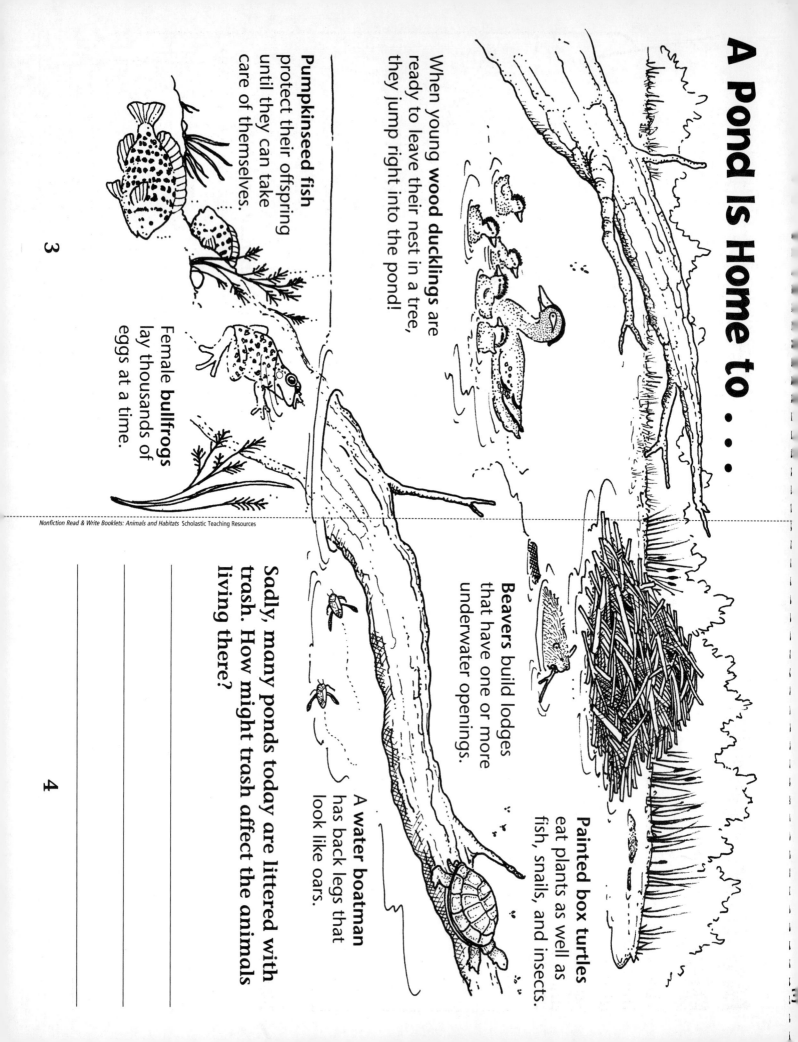

Nonfiction Read & Write Booklets: Animals and Habitats Scholastic Teaching Resources

My Book About Rain Forest Animals

by _____

My Rain Forest Discovery!

There are millions of insect species that live in the rain forest. Many insects have yet to be discovered. Imagine a rain forest insect that you were the first to discover. Draw the insect and describe its diet and habits. Then name the insect after yourself!

Name: _____

7

Tropical Rain Forest Facts

- A tropical rain forest is one of the wettest parts of the world. It is almost always raining in a rain forest.

- Because a rain forest is so wet, more than two out of every three plant species in the world grow here.

- More than half of all the world's animal species live in the rain forest.

1

Choose two types of protection from the web to compare and contrast:

_____ and _____

How are these two methods similar?

_____

_____

_____

_____

How are they different?

_____

_____

_____

_____

_____

6

Rain Forest Song
by Bobbi Katz

Fruits thunk to the forest floor.
Raindrops pitter patter.
Parrots squawk and termites bore.
Monkeys chitter chatter.
Beetles click and lemurs munch.
(Someone's *always* having lunch!)
Mosquitoes whine and bats squeak.
Serpents hiss and branches creak.
Fruits thunk to the forest floor.
Raindrops pitter patter . . .

"Rain Forest Song" Copyright © 1994 by Bobbi Katz.

Below, list other rain forest animals you know.

_____

_____

2

How Rain Forest Animals Protect Themselves

Camouflage
Some animals, like the chameleon, use color to blend into their surroundings. This lets them hide from enemies.

Warn Predators With Colors
Some poisonous animals, like the poison dart frog, warn enemies of their danger with their bright colors.

Scare Predators
Some animals have body features or markings that frighten enemies. The frilled lizard displays a brightly colored flap of skin that makes it look larger.

5

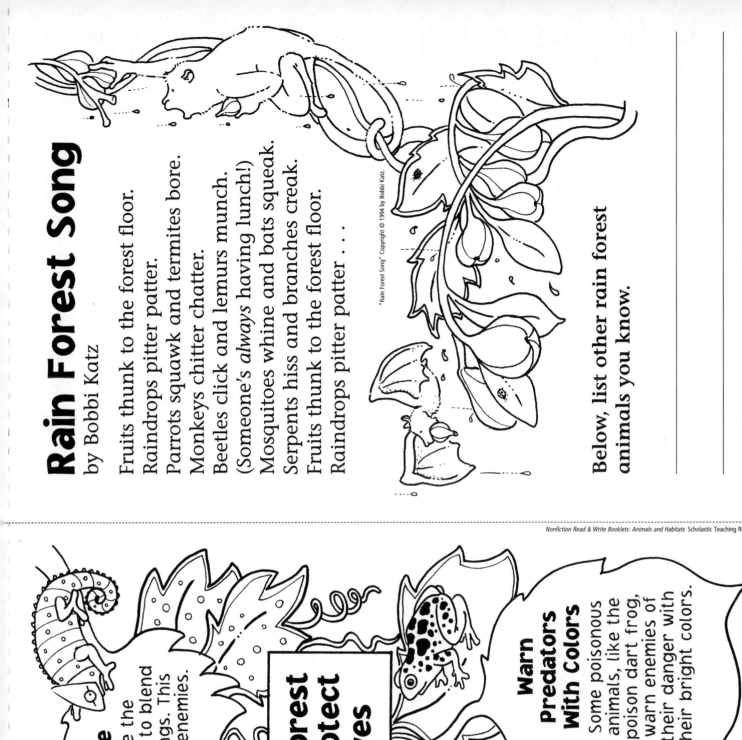

A Tropical Rain Forest

Toucans do not fly very well. Instead, they hop among the trees.

Spider monkeys use their long tails to hang from branches and move quickly through the trees.

Jaguars pounce from trees onto their prey.

What else do you know about these or other rain forest animals?

Nonfiction Read & Write Booklets: Animals and Habitats Scholastic Teaching Resources

Is Home to . . .

Red-eyed tree frogs are nocturnal, or active at night.

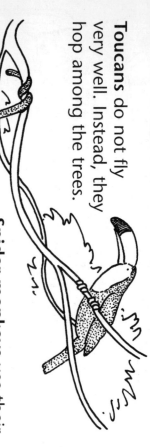

Flying dragons use flaps of skin to glide from tree to tree.

Giant anteaters use their long tongues to catch and eat ants and termites in the ground.

Which animal or animals would you like to learn more about? Why?

My Book About Ocean Animals

by _____

Stay Away, Enemies!

Many ocean animals have special body parts that protect them from enemies. Some have sharp spikes all over their bodies or strong, pinching claws. Others have hard shells or stinging tails. Many have sharp teeth.

Create an imaginary sea creature that uses these or other ways to protect itself. Then describe what your animal does when an enemy approaches.

7

A Wet and Wonderful Home

Did you know . . . ?

- Earth looks blue from space because there is so much water on its surface. Two-thirds of its surface is covered with water.

- The largest areas of seawater are called oceans. Smaller parts of the ocean that are partially enclosed by land are called seas.

- All oceans on Earth flow into one another without borders. You could sail to every ocean without land getting in the way.

- All seawater is salty. Over millions of years, freshwater has picked up salt minerals from rocks and soil and dumped it back into the ocean.

- There are more than one million different kinds of plants and animals that live in the ocean!

1

The shark is another ocean animal in danger. Read about the problem and think about how people might help save sharks.

PROBLEM:
Sharks are hunted for food and for sport. Many sharks are hunted only for their fins, which are used in soup.

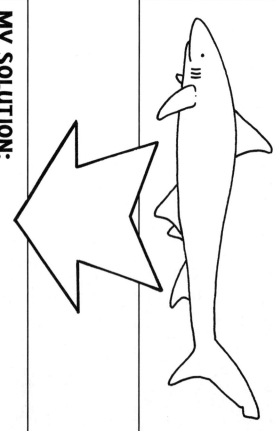

MY SOLUTION:

4

6

Draw a picture of an ocean animal you know something about. Or do research on an ocean animal you'd like to learn more about. Then write some fun facts about this creature.

2

Help!

Many ocean animals are in danger. Read the chart to learn solutions to some problems.

Ocean Animal	Problem	Solution
humpback whale	This whale was hunted for many years for its blubber, or fat. People used the blubber to make oil for lamps.	In 1966, laws were passed to stop the hunting of humpback whales.
brown pelican	A chemical called DDT was used to kill insects that ate crops. Brown pelicans ate the insects and became sick or died.	In 1972, a law was passed that said DDT could no longer be used.
dolphin	Nets that were used to catch tuna fish also caught dolphins. The dolphins often drowned in the nets.	Many people stopped buying tuna until the companies used safer ways to catch fish.

5

Know the Zones!

There are three levels, or zones, in the ocean. The zone names tell how much sunlight reaches each area.

Sunlit Zone

(Sunlight reaches down to about 660 feet.)

Dolphins make friends by stroking each other's flippers.

Twilight Zone

(Light becomes dimmer, reaching from about 660 feet to 3,300 feet deep.)

Hatchet fish have big eyes that help them see in the dim light.

Midnight Zone

(No sunlight reaches below 3,300 feet. The deepest part of the ocean may be more that 35,000 feet deep.)

Gulper eels have huge mouths that allow them to eat fish twice their size.

3

Fish mostly stay in their zone. Why?

The **Portuguese man-of-war** drifts on the surface of the ocean. Its long, stinging tentacles dangle in the water and wait for a meal to swim by.

Humpback whales live in family groups and "talk" to one another by singing long songs.

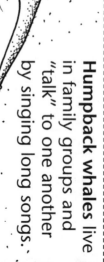

The **deep-sea angler** has a glowing rod on top of its head. Small fish thinks it's food and swim into the angler's large jaws.

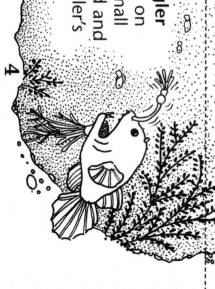

4

My Book About Wetland Animals

by _____

How Hats Hurt the Heron

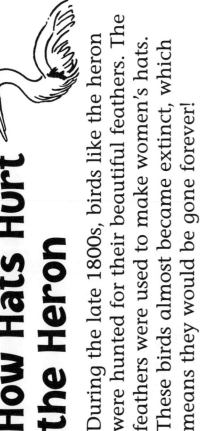

During the late 1800s, birds like the heron were hunted for their beautiful feathers. The feathers were used to make women's hats. These birds almost became extinct, which means they would be gone forever!

Imagine you lived during those times. Create a poster that teaches people about the dangers of hunting birds like the heron. Include a picture on your poster.

7

5

Wetland Fact Wheel

Read the information in the wheel to learn about wetlands.

There are different kinds of wetlands, including marshes, swamps, bogs, sloughs, and fens.

They can have fresh water or salt water.

They are found all over the world, along the shallow edges of rivers, streams, ponds, lakes, and oceans.

WETLANDS

They can be as large as many football fields strung together.

Some stay wet all year. Others are wet only part of the year.

They are home to thousands of plants and animals.

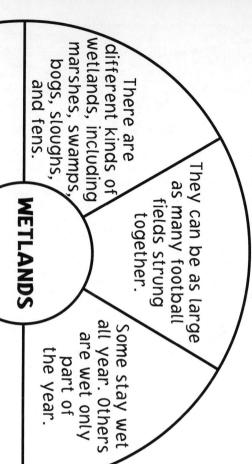

1

Nonfiction Read & Write Booklets: Animals and Habitats Scholastic Teaching Resources

When a wetland is saved . . .

Plants and animals thrive in their unique habitat.

Wetlands help prevent flooding by taking in the extra water.

Tiny wetland bacteria destroy pollutants in our water supply. This makes our water cleaner.

Wetland plants help remove large amounts of carbon dioxide from the air. This makes our air cleaner.

Can you think of another reason to save the wetlands?

_____

6

4

Write a new fact you learned from reading the Wetland Fact Wheel.

_____

Here is a question I have about wetlands:

_____

Here is my prediction for the answer:

_____

2

Nonfiction Read & Write Booklets: Animals and Habitats Scholastic Teaching Resources

Wetland Wonders

Wetlands are important for so many reasons. Read the chart to learn more.

When a wetland is destroyed . . .

1. Thousands of plants and animals lose their home. Many are in danger of dying out forever.

2. More flood control projects need to be built to control the extra floodwater.

3. More water treatment plants need to be built because wetlands are a natural way to clean our water supply.

4. The level of dangerous carbon dioxide gas in the air rises.

5

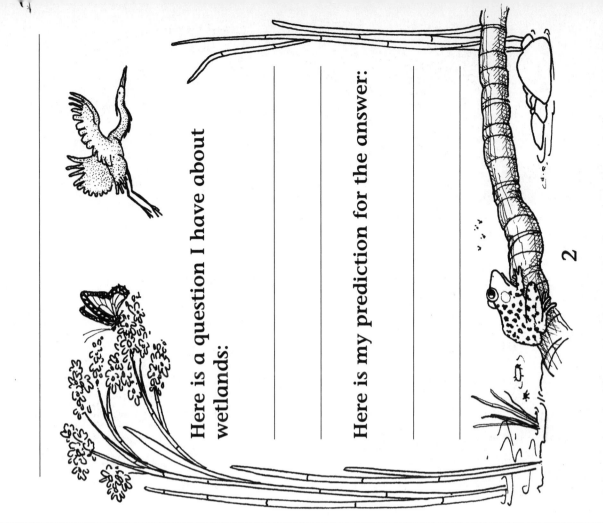

A Swamp Is Home to ...

Great blue herons use their sharp beaks to spear fish.

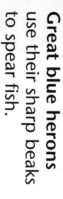

Muskrats collect water plants for their lodge, or home.

Alligators are a top predator in a wetland.

Manatees are gentle mammals that can weigh more than 1,000 pounds.

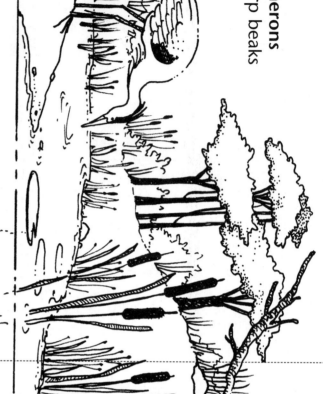

At just two inches long, **mosquito fish** are often eaten by birds and other fish.

Diamondback terrapins use webbed hind feet to propel themselves through water.

Many wetlands have been destroyed to make room for farms, homes, and shopping malls. What do you think happens to wetland animals in these places?

3

4